The Winning Team

A Victory Guide for Total Team Success

Sederick Fluker

WESTBOW
PRESS
A DIVISION OF THOMAS NELSON

WestBow Press books may be ordered through booksellers or by contacting:

WestBow Press
A Division of Thomas Nelson
1663 Liberty Drive
Bloomington, IN 47403
www.westbowpress.com
1-(866) 928-1240

ISBN: 978-1-4497-9400-2 (sc)
ISBN: 978-1-4497-9401-9 (hc)
ISBN: 978-1-4497-9402-6 (e)

Library of Congress Control Number: 2013908009

Printed in the United States of America.

WestBow Press rev. date: 5/28/2013

Table of Contents

Acknowledgments

To my wife: Sametta, you are an amazing supporter of dreams. Thank you for taking this journey with me and being my number-one cheerleader throughout this project. I love you always.

To my children: Serenity and Samiya, it's a joy watching you two grow up. I hope my legacy will inspire you guys to greatness someday. Daddy loves you very much.

To my parents: Mom and Dad, thanks for the unwavering support and unconditional love you've given me since birth. You embody the true essence of a winning team. I love you both.

To my family: I am grateful to my immediate and extended family members. Your support throughout the years has been priceless. I love you all.

To my teachers: Thanks to each of you for your amazing role in laying the foundation for my success in life. I want to especially thank Mrs. Stallworth for teaching me knowledge beyond the books, and Ms. Blair for inspiring me to write.

To my coaches: I appreciate the countless hours you invested in my growth—not just athletic, but also personal. Coach Boykin, you were a standout.

To my publisher: I want to extend special thanks to the team at WestBow Press for an invested commitment to seeing this project completed. From start to finish, your input has been invaluable.

Introduction

One may wonder how a book about winning teams can benefit businesses, school systems, nonprofit entities, company owners, and professionals in the workplace. Considering that most people associate the word "team" with organized sports, it's easy to overlook the application of the team concept to other settings. However, I believe any entity that has a group of people working together to achieve a common goal can be considered a team. And if a team outscores or outperforms its competition in a given period of time, then that team is the *winning* team. Therefore, the winning team concept should not be restricted to sports teams only but should be embraced by any group-entity that desires to be the best it can possibly be. This book will serve as a victory guide to help teams maximize their productivity, enhance their performances, and reach their full potential as champions.

First of all, it's important for team organizations to clearly define winning in their own contexts. This is because winning means different things to different teams. A sports team, for example, obviously wouldn't define a win in the same way as a business team. Because winning can generally be defined by some percentage of measurable success, it can be broadly applied across various team settings. So whether you're part of a Fortune 500 company or part of a little league baseball team, the concepts in this book can help you and your team become winners.

One concept that recurs throughout this book is *total team success*. I believe every individual on a team has a valuable contribution to make to the team's overall success, regardless of how significant or insignificant their role may seem. Total team success is about each person contributing in some way to the team's victory. In the end, the total team must take responsibility for its successes as well as its failures. That's why all members of a team must do their part and do it well if a team is to ultimately win.

I also believe teams have to be formulated and crafted for success. Just as cars are crafted for quality performance, a winning team must be skillfully crafted and properly assembled for the purpose of performing flawlessly as a unit. It's a fallacy to think that a winning team will somehow magically come together. No, winning teams are first designed and then developed over time; it's a process. Therefore, it is important to understand what goes into the making of a winning team.

The ideas I discuss in this book aren't all new; what I've

attempted to do is harness strategies for winning into one comprehensive source. It's a victory guide for teams that are striving to become winners. I'm confident that all win-driven teams will find this book simple, practical, and productive. Enjoy the journey to your success!

1

The Assembly Line: Origins of a Winning Team

In a consumer-driven society much of our focus is product-based rather than process-based. We tend to focus more on results than on how they are actually produced. For instance, most people don't care to know how ice cream is made, but they do care whether it tastes good or is good quality. Similarly, some teams just want winning results, but they dismiss the process that leads to victory. Producing a winning team requires a paradigm shift from a product-based focus to a process-based focus. We must examine the creation of a winning team to make the process purposeful and intentional. It reminds me of a factory assembly line. A factory assembly line consists of several strategic steps and stages designed to produce a finished product. Likewise, assembling a winning team involves a series of strategic steps and stages that all work together to produce victory as the final product. Much of the assembly process involves bringing together individual components. Although each component has a separate, distinct function, the goal of the assembly process is to strategically connect all the components so they can function as one unit. This chapter serves as a theoretical assembly line to help readers connect the most basic elements of the team concept with the processes that work together to produce victory.

Understanding Basic Team Makeup

Before you can begin the process of assembling a winning team, you have to first understand the basic makeup of a team infrastructure. Most teams consist of two primary groups of individuals working together toward a common goal. I will refer to them as *team leaders* and *team workers*, and both groups collectively as *team members*. Team leaders include general managers, coaches, principals, team owners, etc. This particular group is responsible for the aspects of leadership and decision-making, including setting vision, purpose, and overall direction for the team. The second group, team workers, includes employees, players, salesmen, etc. This group is primarily responsible for carrying out various tasks set in motion by the team leaders. Each group can be further divided into primary and secondary groups with similar functions but with different amounts of delegated authority. One example is a head coach and an assistant head coach. One has more delegated authority than the other, but both are part of the team's leadership core. The complexity of having primary and secondary groups inside of an existing team can eventually lead to the formation of *subteams*. These are essentially teams within a team. Regardless of their specific designation, it's important for all team members to collaborate in order to accomplish the team's overall goal.

Fundamentals of Team Building

When it comes to assembling a winning team, many seek to acquire the best individuals they can find. That's perfectly understandable. Who wouldn't want the best individuals on their teams? However, the term "best" shouldn't be relegated only to individuals with the best skill sets or talents on a particular team. No, I believe the best team members are those who *function* best inside of the team concept. This is important when team building because a team functions like any other unit in that one part affects the whole. To illustrate this point, let's consider the human body, which is a unit made up of numerous parts. If a kidney, for instance, doesn't perform adequately, then the rest of the body will be adversely affected. No problem, just replace the kidney, right? It sounds simple enough, but in reality, you can't just take any old kidney and use it as a replacement. No, it has to be the right fit for that particular body. In other words, the chemistry has to be right. The same holds true for a winning team. You can't just implant any old person into the team.

It's very important that the team chemistry be just right in order to produce winning results. A successful team must consist of individuals that gel with each other and work well as a unit. That's why during the interviewing process most employers will ask candidates whether they work well with others. This is a critical component in establishing good team chemistry. Keep in mind that just because a team member works well, it doesn't necessarily mean he or she works well with others. This is why team leaders should take a team-over-talent approach to team building. In other words, they should recruit individuals who are more committed to the overall greatness of the team than to their own individual greatness—then total team success will be inevitable.

Establishing a Winning Team Culture

The world we live in is full of diverse cultures. Cultures are the distinguishing factors that exist among various peoples, groups or entities, including beliefs, values, practices, and behaviors. Teams also have cultures that distinguish them. It's important for team members to infuse their culture with the idea of winning so that it becomes the official language of the team. Everything about a team's culture should say to others: "We are winners"! Additionally, the drive to win must be evident in the core values and performance of each team member. A winning team culture is basically an environmental standard that allows teams to incubate success. For example, there is no such thing as halfheartedly performing assignments; even practice sessions are to be taken seriously. Team members support each other and take collective responsibility for their successes and failures. Also, in a winning team culture, negativity is completely banished in favor of team unity and unwavering passion for total team success. As far as winning is concerned, every team member wants it, speaks it, demonstrates it, cultivates it, and believes it! A winning team culture is like the conveyer belt in the assembly line that propels teams forward in a positive direction toward victory.

Winning Team Synthesis: Exploring the Process

It is fitting to compare an assembly line to a winning team because both have individual components that come together in a series of processes to produce a final product. As we look closer at the process for developing winning teams, we must become familiar with a concept I call *winning team synthesis.* This is the process by which various individual components come together to produce a winning team. The following conceptual model illustrates the key components of winning team synthesis.

Conceptual Model: Winning Team Synthesis

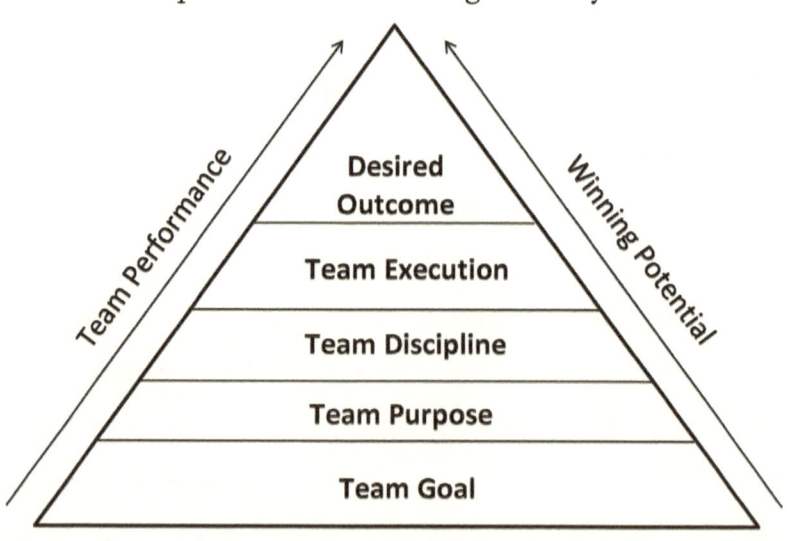

Developed by Sederick Fluker

As you can see, the first component is the team goal. Whether it's winning a trophy, a contest, or a sale's quota, most teams strive to achieve some type of goal. In the case of a winning team, winning itself becomes the goal of the team- not just tangible prizes and awards. When winning itself becomes the goal of a team, numerous prizes and awards are sure to follow! Nevertheless, a team goal should be the unifying mechanism by which all individuals on the team come together to collectively pursue.

Once established, the goal of a team flows right into its purpose. Team purpose is the reason why a particular team exists. It is the thread that weaves individuals together in a common cause. That's why it's important for all teams to have a clearly defined purpose. If a team has no purpose, then it has no reason to exist! A clearly defined team purpose gives rise to team discipline, which is the commitment of all team members to endure the necessary conditions to achieve their goals. Team discipline requires training, sacrifice, self-denial, and self-control from each team member. As a result of discipline, teams should demonstrate consistent execution of desired tasks. Execution is directly related to performance; therefore, as teams execute specific tasks better, they ultimately perform better overall.

When teams consistently execute specific tasks, they

position themselves to achieve the desired outcome. Eventually, the team's goal and its desired outcome should be one and the same. For example, if winning is the team goal, then winning should eventually be the outcome. However, teams must progress through each of the various components of winning team synthesis before success can be achieved.

Finally, the arrows that run along the outer walls of the pyramid in the conceptual model represent the correlation between a team's performance and its winning potential. As a team successfully progresses through each stage of the winning team synthesis, the team's overall performance continuously increases. When a team's overall performance increases, then its winning potential also increases. Since chance is always a factor, there is no exact formula to guarantee a win. However, a team that performs well in a given period of time can significantly increase its chances of winning. I'm convinced that an exceptional performance puts a team in the best possible position to win. Therefore, it's important to consider all of the things that go into producing an exceptional team performance. We will explore some of them more closely in the next chapter. Ultimately, teams should perform in such a way that winning becomes their reality.

2

Winning Traits:
Characteristics of a Winning Team

I can remember sitting in a science class several years ago and being practically bored to death. I was dreading the next concept to be taught when all of a sudden, my science teacher introduced a term that sparked my interest. The term was deoxyribonucleic acid (DNA). I remember thinking that a word that long had to be extremely important, and I was right. I learned that DNA is the genetic material that determines the traits or characteristics (such as eye color, hair texture, height) of living organisms. Perhaps you're wondering what a science lesson about DNA has to do with winning teams. Well, just as the DNA of living organisms is responsible for their visible traits, at the core of every winning team there is winning DNA. The evidence of its existence can be seen in the traits or characteristics of winning teams. They are numerous and distinct and visibly present in teams that win. As we explore these winning traits in the chapter, I challenge teams to compare them to their own characteristics. If a team lacks any of the traits, it should strive to acquire them through developmental strategies, consultations, or other effective vehicles and resources. The basic goal is to possess all of these winning traits with the expectation of seeing winning as an end result. I should mention that although there are possibly some traits not mentioned here, I've highlighted the five traits most commonly shared by winning teams.

Unity

One of the most recognizable characteristics of a winning team is unity. Team unity is the invisible glue that holds a team together. Although teams consist of diverse individuals, the key is for everyone to function as one harmonious unit. Sometimes that's easier said than done, but unity is always prevalent among teams that win. I vividly remember watching a particular basketball game on television one day. After the game was over, I began listening to the postgame interviews of key players from the winning team. It was interesting to note that even after the game was over, these key players continued to exhibit absolute unity. The players never gloated about their own personal accomplishments, but instead gave credit to their team as a whole for the victory. Even when the interviewer tried to get each player to boast about his own individual achievements in the game, the player simply redirected the focus away from himself and placed it back on his teammates. To say these team members were on the same page is an understatement. No, they were unified; they were one! This kind of unity is essential for winning teams. In fact, unity should be embedded in the fabric of every team's culture. Team members must also play an active role in deterring selfish ambitions, which work against team unity. The focus should always remain on the team and on keeping it strong. Teams must protect unity by discouraging any behavior, attitude, or action that threatens it. Now, don't get me wrong. There's nothing wrong with acknowledging individuality or even individual greatness, as long as it doesn't devalue the contributions of others on the team. If any individual player is to boast, it should be about the collective efforts of his or her teammates. This type of selfless posture helps to reinforce team unity. So what if a running back rushes 1,000 yards in a season? It was the offensive lineman who blocked opponents and opened up lanes for him to run through! So what if a point guard scores over thirty points in a basketball game? It was the center who blocked shots, got rebounds, and prevented opponents from scoring more points. My point is that it takes a unified team effort to win. Everyone on a team should contribute to a victory in some way. Even the supporting cast of players on the sideline or bench has an important role to play in a team's victory. That's why I call it total team success, and team unity is a big part of that success!

Consistency of Execution

You've probably heard the expression "practice makes perfect." Although perfection is an elusive goal to define, I believe this phrase embodies another important characteristic of winning teams: *consistency of execution.* Let's analyze the expression. We know that practice is generally routine exercise a person does in order to improve a particular skill or the consistency of executing that skill in a performance situation. For example, why might a basketball player practice shooting baskets from a free throw line hundreds of times? It's because he or she wants to perfect the craft of shooting free throws through practice, thereby shooting a higher percentage of free throws in a real game. Therefore, the goal of practice is to perfect or be able to consistently execute a desired task when it's needed.

This is an important principle to grasp because many good teams have lost to lesser opponents simply because of inconsistency in executing certain tasks when they were needed in a performance or contest situation. Therefore, teams that have a greater consistency of execution will have a greater chance of winning in a competition.

Sports teams aren't the only beneficiaries of this concept. Business teams must also consistently execute specific tasks within their organizations to be successful. Those tasks are usually to provide a quality product or service to consumers. Because of the competitive venue many business teams operate in, consistency of execution can make the difference between staying on top of the competition and staying at the bottom of it. Most consumers expect companies to deliver their desired products or services with unwavering consistency. For example, when a great steak restaurant first opened up in my area, my wife and I decided to dine there, and we thoroughly enjoyed two delicious steaks. However, the next time we dined there, we didn't get the same quality of steak that first lured us to the establishment. Needless to say, we were very disappointed and didn't do business with them again. Maybe the cooking team was having an off night. Who knows? All it takes is one off night for a team to lose to its competition. Remember, consistency of execution leads to better team performance, and better team performance is the doorway to victory over the competition.

Successful team-based companies, especially international ones, understand the importance of consistency. For example, let's consider the McDonald's corporation. Have you ever noticed that you can order a menu item from a McDonald's restaurant in one geographic location and it will taste virtually the same as one you order from another McDonald's halfway around the world? The same holds true for other large fast food chains. This is because the team members of those entities consistently execute the plan put in place by the company's leadership. It doesn't matter if team members are executing a recipe book or a playbook; when it's done consistently, they position themselves to be victorious in most performance situations.

Now, this is where things can get a bit tricky. Just having the right plan in place doesn't guarantee that it will be executed consistently. Therefore, it's important for teams to not only have the right plan in place, but also to have the right *people* in place to execute the plan. Additionally, all team members, especially those in leadership, must have good accountability. Inadequate leadership can affect the execution and overall performance of a team organization. At other times, team workers might not be efficient in executing their assigned tasks. Whatever the case, consistency of execution is needed from all team members, both individually and collectively, to ensure the kind of team performance that leads to victory.

Synergy

Not every team has synergy, but a winning team will always have synergy! Synergy is the cooperative interaction of two or more agents so that their combined effect is greater than the sum of their individual effects. This definition contains important insight about the role of synergy in a winning team. The first important component of synergy is *cooperative interaction*. Cooperative interaction comes about when everyone on the team has bought into the idea that "Together, we can." The realization that each team member is valuable to achieving total team success is the necessary fuel for cooperative interaction. In contrast, selfishness and an inability to cooperate with fellow teammates will destroy the synergy of a team. What I've learned over the years is that while some individuals work well, they don't always work well with others! Nevertheless, it's important for team members to gel, interact, and work together in one harmonious spirit of cooperation. When this takes place, the team becomes infused with a contagious, unified energy—what we refer to as synergy. I have often wondered what team members mean when, in describing an exceptional team performance, they make the statement, "We feed off each other." I now believe this is a simple description of synergy that comes from cooperative interaction. Synergistic teams are capable of performing at higher levels of efficiency due to their cooperative interaction. This high efficiency in performance is also a byproduct of the other important component of synergy, the *combined effect*. The combined effect can be summarized by an adopted acronym for team: **T**ogether, **E**veryone **A**chieves **M**ore. This is certainly true of synergistic teams that excel in performance due to the combined efforts of each team member. In my earlier years of playing organized sports, my old baseball coach used to always shout, "You've got help!" This reminded each of us as players to rely on our collective abilities to produce an exceptional team performance. For instance, if our pitcher began to throw wild pitches in an effort to win the game off his own arm, the coach would shout, "You've got help!" to remind our pitcher that he had teammates who could provide the necessary defense if batters hit his pitches into the field of play. Knowingly or not, the coach strengthened the synergy of our team, and because of our combined effect, we reigned as league champions for several years. This example is a reminder that everyone on a team plays a valuable part in winning, and the combined effort of a team is greater than the individual efforts of its members. Too often we've seen how a talented player can score the majority of a team's points, and that particular team still loses. However, a synergistic team fosters an environment conducive for total team contribution towards a victory. Unlikely heroes will often emerge to propel a team to victory when synergy is present. This is why I believe synergy is one of the most essential traits of winning teams and the foundation for total team success.

Exceptional Performance

Everything that goes into a team, good or bad, all culminates into a single performance or series of performances. It doesn't matter how great a team is perceived to be; it doesn't matter how talented the team members are; it doesn't even matter if the team has a winning history. The only thing that matters is how well the team performs when given the opportunity. A team must be able to outperform its competition in a given period of time in order to be declared the winning team. Therefore, winning teams must generate exceptional performances on demand. An exceptional performance is what separates good teams from great teams, and great teams from winning teams. Even an underdog team can defeat a heavily favored team by giving an exceptional performance. However, this doesn't happen haphazardly. There are three important factors that go into the making of an exceptional team performance: time, opportunity, and execution.

Let's begin with time. All teams will be confronted with two categories of time: preparation time and performance time. Preparation time has to do with the time allotted for a team to prepare for a contest or competition. Preparation time includes drills, practices, simulations, scrimmages, etc. Teams must use their preparation time to improve weaknesses and build upon strengths. Once a team has properly utilized its preparation time, it must take advantage of its performance time. Performance time is the set amount of time allotted for teams to perform during a contest. Teams that perform well understand the importance of managing time and using it to their advantage in competition. Time can be a team's best friend or its worst enemy. Therefore, time management is critical both in preparation and during an actual performance.

Another factor of exceptional team performance is opportunity. Team contests are full of opportunities. An exceptional performance is based on the number of opportunities seized by a team; this usually translates into a number of missed opportunities for the opposing team. Therefore, it is important for the team unit as well as for each individual team member to seize his or her own moments of opportunity.

The last factor that contributes to exceptional team performance is execution. Execution has to do with carrying out specific tasks during critical moments of competition; in short, it is doing all the right things at the right time. As stated earlier, teams must *consistently* execute important tasks for the duration of a competition. This definitely requires solid individual performances from team members. Another way of looking at it is that exceptional team performances are made possible by exceptional individual performances. In any case, teams with pockets of inconsistency and poor execution will find it difficult to capture a win when needed.

Exceptional team performance might be summarized by the following equation:

Good Time Management + Seized Opportunities + Consistent Execution = Exceptional Performance

Strong Leadership

It is my belief that strong teams require strong leaders. Strong leadership is crucial to the success of any team desiring to win. It doesn't matter how much talent a team is stocked with; the standing leadership of that team must be able to pull all of the team's elements and dynamics together to function as one effective unit. Winning teams seldom have passive leadership. They have assertive leaders who can take the bull by the horns in order to get maximum productivity from their teams. Strong leadership is also responsible leadership. This means that leaders don't shift the responsibility or blame for performance outcomes onto others. Instead, they take full responsibility for both exceptional and poor team performances. Additionally, strong leaders stand by their decisions whether they are viewed favorably or not. Weak leaders are the exact opposite; they have no place in the scheme of a winning team. A team equipped with the right workers but lacking strong leadership is destined to lose. That's why a change in team leadership is often needed to reflect a change in team results. I want to challenge you to observe how things operate the next time you visit a place of business, school, or organization. If that particular entity operates with a spirit of excellence, then it is likely the result of strong leadership in the organization. On the other hand, if there's poor service, poor performance, and poor accountability, that is most likely the result of weak leadership. I'm sure many of us have personally witnessed the effects of both strong and weak leadership on teams. Interestingly enough, strong leaders can elicit maximum productivity from a group of individuals, whereas weak leaders can cause the overall productivity and performance of the same group of individuals to decline. That's why teams must evaluate the performances of all its members, including team leaders, to determine the source of performance problems. I think too many teams make the mistake of inadvertently blaming team workers for performance-related issues really caused by deficiencies in leadership. Moreover, teams must exercise good judgment when appointing individuals to leadership roles. Strong and good leadership should be synonymous with winning teams. I believe in this principle so much that I've dedicated an entire chapter to the importance of leadership and the role it plays in winning teams.

3

The Right Stuff: The Role of Leadership in Winning Teams

For winning teams, having the right stuff is more than a notion, more than a cliché, and definitely more than the title of a book and movie about astronauts. I believe the right stuff is having dynamic team leadership that propels a team to victory. The role of leadership is significant and vital to the success of any team. With that in mind, let us closely examine leadership and the role it plays in producing winning teams. There is a lot of literature and many materials available to help teams and individuals develop good leadership, so I myself will not be taking the liberty of exploring in-depth analyses of specific leadership types, styles, or personalities. Instead, in this chapter I want to explore various leadership models prevalent among successful teams. Each of these leadership models plays an important role; they should be adopted by leaders and used in combination to produce exceptional team performances. Five leadership models are reviewed in this chapter.

Motivational Leadership

It can be very unsettling trying to lead a team to victory when its members aren't motivated to give their best effort. There could be numerous reasons why team members lack motivation to perform at the desired and expected level, but it is the tedious task of the team leader to find a method, or *motivation factor*, to motivate the entire team to perform at the highest level possible. In fact, there are three motivation factors a team leader can use to enhance both individual and group performances in a team: rewards, rank, and recognition.

First of all, let's consider rewards. Rewards are frequently used as motivational tools. A large company may give away millions of dollars in bonuses each year because bonuses serve as a reward to motivate team members to do their best work for the company. The good part about using rewards is that they can be varied. Whether it's a pay raise, a trophy, special privileges, or incentives, rewards are effective in motivating team members. Rewards don't have to be large or expensive either. They simply have to motivate people to maximize their full potential on behalf of the team. Every team member has a motivation factor. The key is for the team leader to find out what motivates his or her team members.

The second motivation factor to consider is rank, which is a certain position or status. A predetermined amount of authority is given to ranked individuals on a team. Team members are often motivated when given the opportunity to achieve a higher status or rank within their organization. Rank can exist in several different forms, such as a lead teacher at a school, a sales manager, a section leader in a band, or a team captain. The pursuit of a particular rank often serves as motivation for team members to do their best work on behalf of the team.

However, team leaders must also be aware that using rank can generate competition among team members. This intra-team competitiveness is often referred to as "friendly competition." The key is to keep it friendly! In other words, competition for rank is fine as long as it does not cause division between team members. That's why team leaders should take the lead in promoting team unity amid rank competitions. This is primarily achieved by emphasizing the importance of everyone's contribution to the team, regardless of rank. If used properly, rank can be a powerful motivator for team members to give their best effort on behalf of their team.

The third motivation factor is recognition. Recognition is a way to say to team members, "We value you and appreciate you!" This in turn becomes a booster shot of motivation for team members. Several years ago when I was working as an educator, a colleague shared with me his frustrations about the principal of his school. The colleague felt discouraged in his job because his principal never acknowledged any of his hard work as a teacher. He stayed after school every week to help struggling students and always went the extra mile to execute tasks assigned to him by the principal. The colleague wanted to continue being a team player but couldn't understand why he never got any recognition for the exceptional work he performed. This story is a reminder that there are some team members who don't need a reward or a special rank to motivate them; all they need is recognition! Sometimes people just want to be noticed. Even if it's a simple pat on the back or praise for a job well done, recognition is a powerful motivating tool. Recognition doesn't cost anything, but it's priceless when used inside of the team concept. When team members are recognized for various accomplishments, it reinforces their value and importance to the team. It also reenergizes their commitment to work harder and better. That's why it's so important for team leaders to learn what motivates their team workers.

The beauty of the three motivation factors is that each one can stand alone as a motivational tool, or they can be used in combination with each other. For example, a team member can be recognized for his or her accomplishments while receiving an award. Or a team member could receive an award for obtaining a particular rank in the organization. In some instances, all three motivation factors can be utilized simultaneously. At the end of the day, it's not about the method; it's about the motivation, and team leaders must employ the necessary tools of motivation to maintain a performance edge over other competitors.

Interpersonal Leadership

Relationship-building is one of the most powerful and underrated occurrences that takes place within a team. Team leaders who forge solid interpersonal relationships with team workers will experience greater levels of commitment and productivity from workers in return. This truth really resonated with me after I watched a few episodes of the television series "Undercover Boss" in which the leaders of companies go undercover to work alongside subordinates in the company. The most impactful aspect of the show was the interpersonal relationships the bosses established with their unassuming workers. These interpersonal relationships, built on trust, allowed the undercover bosses to hear firsthand about the challenges of team workers in performing their jobs. Once the true identity of an undercover boss is revealed, the workers are typically overwhelmed with gratitude for the boss's caring, listening, encouraging, and having genuine concern for them. As a result, many of the organizations experienced greater commitment, productivity, and performance from their team workers afterward. This echoes a popular cliché: "People don't care how much you know until they know how much you care." It's important for all team members to know that they are valued and considered important as people first.

Sometimes, team leaders can become so driven by results that they ignore some of the basic human needs of their team workers. They essentially become *impersonal managers* rather than interpersonal leaders. Impersonal managers are often task-oriented and program-driven. In contrast, interpersonal leaders have a people-over-program philosophy. This means that people always come first. These leaders realize that it doesn't matter how good a team's program may be; the program can only be as good as the people who facilitate it. I have a theory, and it's simple: take good care of your people, and your people will take good care of you. That's why it's important for team leaders to stay abreast of the individual and collective needs of their team workers. Because a team is made up of a diverse group of individuals, there could be a number of issues including personality conflicts that can adversely affect a team's performance. Therefore, a team leader must be *relationally relevant* to his or her workers in order to successfully navigate them through individual and corporate challenges.

It's important for team leaders to cultivate solid, interpersonal relationships. One of the best ways of doing this is by simply listening. Team workers generally want to be listened to. They don't want unilateral decision making or for team leaders to grant their every wish; most team workers just want to know that they have a voice on the team and that their input is valued regardless of the final decisions made by team leaders. Totally dismissing input from team workers, though, will cause them to eventually shut down. As a result, the team may exhibit an overall decline in morale. Low team morale leads to low team contribution, and low team contribution leads to low team productivity. Low team productivity leads to low team performance, and low team performance will lead to a team's defeat. This is why many interpersonal leaders have an open-door policy for accepting input and feedback from their workers. This helps to close communication gaps while building a positive working alliance between team leaders and team workers—a must for winning teams.

Assertive Leadership

One day in grad school, there was a class discussion about how to deal with difficult people at work. As my peers began sharing their personal encounters with difficult people, the room began to stir with raw, unleashed emotions. After the emotional catharsis ended, the professor politely informed us that dealing with difficult people will often involve confronting them. That was a very unsettling notion at the time, especially for those of us who naturally shied away from confrontation. The professor took the opportunity to introduce to us the concept of assertiveness. She convinced us that we all needed assertiveness training. She said, "You have to learn to be assertive, especially if you want to be great leaders someday. When you're assertive, you can look people in the eye and tell them that you disapprove of their actions while keeping a straight face; you don't have to show anger, raise your voice, or lose any sleep." Finally, the professor insisted that each of us practice being assertive by role-playing. That simple exercise revolutionized my life and my leadership potential. It is my belief that some of the most successful team leaders are those who provide assertive leadership, that is, confident and bold leadership.

Again, strong teams require strong leaders. Leadership should never be weak, passive, or unintentional. Assertive leaders are proactive in navigating their teams to success. Part of that navigation to success involves dealing assertively with challenging people and circumstances. Because teams will include people with varying personalities, egos, agendas, and opinions, team leaders must be assertive in maintaining a team culture in which diversity is respected, but team unity is preserved at all costs. Additionally, assertive leaders understand the need to be secure in their own leadership capacities. Insecure team leaders will often stifle the growth of their teams because of their own insecurities. They will also muffle creativity, individuality, and any other uncontrolled, unpredictable facets of the team. They are often control freaks who fear losing control over situations. Assertive leaders are the exact opposite. They remain secure and confident in their ability to lead.

I've found that assertive leadership is definitely needed

when dealing with two distinct types of people: different people and difficult people. Let's be clear. Being different doesn't necessarily equate to being difficult. Just because a person thinks independently or appears to be overly confident doesn't mean he or she is trying to undermine the team. There will always be team members who have different point of views, opinions, mindsets, values, and habits, yet they love their team and enjoy contributing positively to its success. On the other hand, difficult people are just that: difficult! They pose a constant threat to the progress of a team. Difficult people have a negative outlook and indulge in self-absorbed behaviors that jeopardize the synergy of a team. Nevertheless, an assertive leader has the ability to handle both different and difficult people. Assertive leaders know how to be confrontational without being controversial. This is accomplished by respecting all individuals on the team while holding each one accountable for operating inside of the team structure.

Finally, I love the fact that assertive leaders remain engaged in the leadership of their teams. It doesn't matter how talented or highly qualified their subordinates may be; assertive leaders never pass off the responsibility of leading. No, they emphatically understand that the buck starts and stops with them.

Indigenous Leadership

In sports you've probably heard certain players referred to as "coaches on the field." This refers to selected players who emerge from within a team to function as secondary team leaders. This process is called indigenous leadership development. Indigenous leadership produces secondary leaders from within a team. Having received mentoring and training, secondary team leaders function as an extension of primary team leaders. Let's say a football team's defensive coordinator functions as the primary team leader for the defensive line. This means he or she is responsible for calling the shots on defense during a game. Nevertheless, a defensive coordinator will often defer to a capable defensive player who functions as a secondary team leader. In other words, the defensive player is trained how to think, act, respond, and make decisions on behalf of the defensive coordinator while on the field of play. This example describes indigenous leadership development.

Again, indigenous leadership has to do with the development of secondary leaders from within a team. I want to stress *from within* because I believe some of the best leaders are those who develop indigenously or from within a particular team organization. It is my belief that these individuals generally understand their team's concept and philosophy for winning better than someone brought in from the outside. I make this premise based on the fact that it takes time to learn how any system operates. Individuals who spend a lot of time observing, learning, and functioning within a team's system have an advantage over those who are totally foreign to that same system. I believe it's wise to explore all possibilities within a team before bringing in someone from the outside to play a prominent role in leading the team. The key is finding the right individual(s) on your team to develop as indigenous secondary leaders. There are some important traits to consider before investing time and energy in a potential secondary leader.

- **Positive Attitude**: A leader must have a positive attitude toward the team as a whole. Researchers suggest that a good attitude is one of the main contributing factors to success. Attitudes are very infectious, whether they are good or bad. Therefore, potential secondary leaders must demonstrate a positive attitude at all times.

- **Teachable Spirit**: All potential secondary leaders must be willing to listen to and learn from their primary team leaders. In other words, they must have teachable spirits. Team members who are talented but not teachable are often destructive forces to themselves and to their teams. One must remember that every leader was once a follower, and every teacher was once a student. No matter how good one's talent, learning never stops! There's always room for improvement. Having a teachable spirit often makes the difference between a good team member and an exceptional team member.

- **Positive Influence**: Leadership will always involve a degree of influence. Potential secondary leaders must have a positive influence on fellow teammates. This includes modeling the correct attitude, behavior, work ethic, and commitment to the goals and objectives of a particular team. This type of positive influence will help to build team synergy while inflating the overall spirit and performance of a team.

- **Reliable**: I think it should go without saying that potential secondary leaders must be reliable. Primary leaders need individuals they can count on when everything's on the line. It's hard to rely on individuals who are consistently inconsistent! If team leaders have to guess whether or not a team member will consistently be on time, perform well, carry out assignments, or show up for training or practice, then he or she is probably not a reliable pick for the position.

- **Loyal**: Loyalty is a must-have for potential secondary leaders. Leaders who are not loyal to their teams can knowingly or unknowingly impede progress. They can also negatively influence the loyalty of other team members. Therefore, it's important to select individuals of good character to lead a team. Individuals of good character will be 100 percent loyal and devoted to the team even if they disagree with certain decisions made by senior leadership. Finally, if a team member wants to be on another team, then grant his or her request! It is difficult for people to be loyal to a team when they have divided hearts.

- **Unselfish**: Potential secondary leaders must exhibit what many in the sports world call unselfish play. In other words, secondary leaders must always put their team before themselves. Even when his or her individual effort is celebrated, a secondary leader must shift the focus back onto total team success. The team's identity must not rest on the shoulders of one ego; the team's collective identity should rest on the total contribution of all who comprise the team. All secondary leaders must understand this concept and keep themselves, as well as their teammates, away from self-centered actions that would impede the progress of the overall team.

These are just a few valuable traits to consider when selecting potential secondary leaders, although there are probably more.

Servant Leadership

Leadership encompasses many things. If we asked a group of people to describe in one word what leadership is, then I'm sure the responses would be varied. Some would probably be words like power, control, influence, example, or strength. However, the word that comes to my mind is *perception*. The perception of one's leadership is critical in getting individuals on a team to do their best. I think it's hard for most people to follow leaders they view negatively, and one of the worst ways a leader can be perceived is as self-absorbed or self-serving. People generally want to follow leaders who have the team's best interests at heart, not leaders who use their teams for personal profit. Team leaders must be willing to lay down their personal ambitions to build solidarity among team members. One of the ways this is done is by demonstrating servant leadership. This is a leadership model that focuses on serving the needs of others on the team. Servant leaders understand the importance of connecting with team workers to facilitate a shared approach to winning. Additionally, they know how to shift the focus away from themselves and place it on achieving team goals. The thing I love most about servant leaders is how they provide an exemplary template for the rest of the team to follow. This is critical because the spirit of a team's leadership is often contagious. In other words, selfish leaders can pass selfishness on to their team workers. Likewise, servant leaders can pass on the spirit of serving to their team workers.

In any case, the actions and attitudes of team members often reflect their leadership. That's why servant leaders have a tremendous opportunity to reinforce selfless service amidst achieving total team success. Just for clarity, servant leaders aren't pushovers. They are definitely in charge of their teams, although they choose not to use intimidation or fear to get maximum productivity from their team workers. Instead, they build relationships with team workers founded on trust and accountability, which facilitates exceptional performances. Servant leaders are also good administrators, not just managers. They know how to be hands-on without micromanaging, and they seldom ask their team workers to do anything they wouldn't be willing to do themselves. For instance, if the team's facility needs cleaning, a servant leader isn't above cleaning it, even if it's not his/her job. The basic point of servant leadership is to model the type of effort and unyielding commitment to the team that breeds personal and corporate success.

4

Demolition Crew:
Destroyers of the Team

Thus far we've been exploring what goes into the making of a winning team. However, we can't fully explore the construction of a winning team without also exploring the things that can destroy a team. There are several things whose counterproductive effects can destroy teams. These team destroyers are what I collectively call the *demolition crew*, and they are detailed extensively in this chapter. My purpose is not to relish in negativity but to bring awareness of these imminent threats to the team concept. Part of being a strong team is safeguarding against weaknesses and potential team destroyers. With that in mind let's explore some team destroyers with the objective of preventing or minimizing their negative effects on positive team growth and productivity.

The Superstar

It's a fact that all stars shine; however, there will inevitably be stars that shine brighter than all the rest. In the context of a team, there are some individuals who shine more brightly than others on the team. Sometimes they are referred to as *superstars*. Superstars are individuals who are admired for having some exceptional talent or ability. Regardless of their skill set, I believe superstars are nothing more than average individuals who consistently do above-average things. In other words, these individuals are efficient at delivering what their team needs, especially in crucial situations. This type of efficiency is what makes superstars stand out, or shine. Most superstars are revered by fellow teammates as the leaders of their particular teams; they might even be referred to as the go-to people of the team. Superstars undeniably add value to certain teams—especially the struggling ones. However, superstars can also be problematic or even destructive to teams if they are not handled properly.

First, we must remember there is always potential for jealousy and resentment among teammates when one of their own is distinctly recognized as the superstar of the team. As if that's not challenging enough, some superstars have a distorted perception that the entire team orbits around them and their egos. Worst of all, coaches and other team leaders often cater to superstars or waive team standards in their favor for fear of losing their talents. As a result, some superstars hold their teams hostage for the use of their extraordinary talents. That's why strong leadership is critical when handling superstars. The job of the leadership is to remind everyone on the team, including the superstar, that nothing is more important than the team itself and maintaining the unity of the team. In order to achieve total team success, the focus must always be on the contributions of everyone—not just the superstar. That's why "team over talent" must consistently be the creed of every team that desires to become a winning team.

Now, don't get me wrong. I believe a superstar and a strong team concept can coexist. Furthermore, I believe superstars should definitely shine as long as their shining brings illumination to the entire team and not just to themselves. Finally, individual talents and egos are expendable, but the team concept and winning can never be expendable.

Star Wars

I'm sure that for many readers, images of intergalactic battles between good and evil are synonymous with the movie title

Star Wars. However, many teams experience their very own star wars but with a much different plot. Team star wars occur when two or more prominent stars on the same team battle for supremacy to become the top star of the team. Team star wars are often seen in professional sports. The scenario generally begins when the reigning superstar of a team, usually a veteran, encounters a new, rising superstar. Although team members look to the veteran star for leadership, it's undeniable that the novice star brings excitement and contributes to winning in a big way. If both stars agree to work together and share the spotlight, then the entire team will likely benefit from this alliance of stars. However, if the stars choose to battle one another in a selfish display of talents and skills, then the rest of the team will be negatively affected. Perhaps the biggest reason star wars are so destructive is because they take focus off the team as a whole and place it on select individuals. In reality, individual performance is only a small part of winning. The team collective must perform well to have a chance of winning any contest. No matter which star wins the war of supremacy, he or she will still need the help of a supporting cast of team members to win over the competition. That's why preserving team unity is far more important than preserving individual egos. I don't care how good a team member may be—he or she can only fulfill one role at a time. On a basketball team, one player can't play all five positions simultaneously. That's why star wars on a team is pretty ridiculous considering that everyone will eventually have to work together to defeat the competition.

Hidden Agendas

Ideally, everyone on a team would be fully committed to the team and to accomplishing its goals. Unfortunately, that's not always the case. Sometimes team members have other plans that take precedence over their commitment to the team. When these are withheld from the rest of the team, they are referred to as *hidden agendas*. Like most team destroyers, hidden agendas take focus away from what's best for the team and instead place it on what's best for select individuals. Thus, hidden agendas are usually initiated by individuals on a team who have ulterior motives. For example, a person may join a team under the pretense of helping it to become successful, hiding the fact that he or she is really joining the team just to build up his or her own personal portfolio or status.

Hidden agendas can also occur when individuals become covertly displeased with issues pertaining to their teams. The inability of team members to openly communicate these issues, for whatever reason, will often lead to the formation of destructive hidden agendas. Sometimes, jealousy among team members who covet each other's positions can provide fuel for hidden agendas. On occasion, disgruntled team members unite in a secret plot to undermine or embarrass the team's leadership by intentionally giving a poor performance.

I suppose if there's an upside to hidden agendas, it's that most of them eventually surface. Sometimes they surface in the form of thoughts and conversations. They may even surface through a person's actions or demeanor. In either case, communication is the best defense against hidden agendas. We can only address the issues that we know about. We simply can't read the minds of fellow team members; we can only hope that everyone has the motive and intent to help the team become successful. In reality, there is always potential for outside special interests to influence individuals on a team. That's why I believe it's important to know at all times what fellow team members are thinking, feeling, saying, and believing about the team and their roles on the team. In fact, it's not a bad idea to periodically survey team members. This allows them an opportunity to anonymously express their current beliefs, feelings, or concerns. Additionally, it helps deter hidden agendas and ultimately alleviate divisive undercurrents that are counterproductive to a team's progress.

Contracts

Professional or business-oriented teams are often confronted with binding legal agreements referred to as *contracts*. Contracts exist between a team organization and its members and are established to protect all parties involved from negligent acts, unfairness, and abuse. Contracts can be helpful tools when implemented properly. On the other hand, contracts can be nightmarish for teams that are locked into agreements with inadequate team members. All too often, a team doesn't realize it has acquired an ineffective, low-performing team member until after having entered into a contract with that individual. And because of the legalities involved with most contracts, these low-performing team members can remain on the team and greatly damage it before due process can take place to remove them. In this case, contracts aren't necessarily bad for individuals; they just aren't always good for teams—especially when contracts provide extended shelter for low-performing team members. This scenario is one of the main reasons why tenure for educators is such a contentious debate.

It's crucial for teams to do thorough background checks on prospective team members prior to establishing contracts with them. Thus it's important to know the history of those who join your team. For instance, does the prospective team member have a history of not cooperating with others? Does he or she have a history of tardiness or excessive absences? These and other questions pertaining to a prospect's history should be explored before finalizing a contract. I have to be honest though: even with all of the precautions teams can put in place to ensure quality individuals join their teams, there is still a possibility of acquiring individuals who slide under the radar, so to speak. Prospective team members will often put their best foot forward in efforts to land a position on a team but don't always perform up to the level of expectancy.

Once a contract has been established, though, the team's leadership can only determine the best way to deal with low-performing team members. First of all, I believe it's important to communicate performance expectations and implement corrective strategies to determine if these poor performances can be remedied. If those corrective efforts fail, then it may become necessary to remove those individuals for the well-being of the team as a whole. If that's the case, then prior to dismissing a contracted team member, team leaders must consider the following options: 1) buy out the team member's contract, 2) do not renew the team member's contract upon expiration, 3) transfer or trade the team member to another team, or 4) build a case for terminating the team member's contract. In any case, legal consultation should be considered before altering a team member's contract. At the end of day, no individual should occupy a team position simply to fulfill a pending contract.

I believe team members should be positive, passionate, and productive when committing to prospective teams. Finally, I'm not against the job security provided by contracts; I just believe that team security should be the top priority when building a winning team.

Politics

Most teams will ultimately be confronted with some element of *politics*. In the context of teams, politics refers to the influences of outside entities attempting to control internal team affairs like decision-making and outcomes. People also refer to politics as "the meeting after the meeting." In many instances, it's probably the meeting before the meeting, too! Both are adequate descriptions of how outside influences and individuals attempt to impose their will on the internal affairs of a team. Politics and hidden agendas tend to go hand in hand. Additionally, politics is usually steeped in selfish ambitions and have little to do with doing what's best for the team.

Let's suppose two athletes are competing for the same starting position on a team. It's obvious to the coach and every player on the team who the best person is for the job. At face value it would seem as if the coach has an easy decision to make. However, what people can't see behind the scenes is the fact that one of the competing athletes has wealthy parents who frequently donate money to benefit the team. These boosters have privately expressed to the coach their eagerness to see their child have the starting position. Finally, these parents have hinted in so many words that they would withdraw their financial support if their child didn't get the starting position. With political precision, these parents have now forced the team's leadership to choose between what's politically correct and what's best for the team. If winning is the objective, then the team's leadership must have the courage to make the decision in the best interest of the team, even if it means standing up to political pressures.

Another example of the effect of politics on teams can be seen by observing our own political system here in America. As we know, elected officials are supposed to work together as one harmonious group of team members representing Team America. However, the system through which we elect public officials is largely bipartisan, which for some translates into loyalty to a political party rather than to the country itself. Sadly enough, politicians often collapse under the immense pressure placed on them to conform to their own political party's agenda or to other outside special interest groups. It's disheartening when crucial decisions are based on what's politically correct instead of logic or doing the right thing. Furthermore, as these political chess matches play out before us daily, some countries are unifying their efforts to challenge our nation's winning legacy of dominance in the world. At the time that I am writing this book, many countries are beginning to surpass the United States in areas such as math, science, and technology. Perhaps we should use our collective energies to compete with other nations instead of to perpetuate divisiveness through our own political civil wars within Team America.

In sports, offensive and defensive teams that are a part of the same team seldom see each other as archenemies. They will often scrimmage against one another to improve each other's weaknesses, not to exploit them. It's important to note that whenever subteams are created within a particular team, the team as a whole must remain unified and free of politics—especially the kind that fuel internal disputes between team members. Bickering among team members only impedes the progress of a team. A team can never be truly effective if it's always divided against itself. For this reason, I believe politics is one of the most destructive forces to the progress of any team. Its damaging effects can only be prevented by unified team members who have enough courage and moral fortitude to act on the side of right in the face of political pressures.

Outside Distractions

Whether private or public, good or bad, there will always be issues affecting individuals on a team. Most of these issues are not directly related to the team itself, but they can affect the entire team due to the interconnectedness of individuals on the team. These issues are fittingly referred to as *outside distractions*. Outside distractions can be numerous and varied. They can also be mild or severe. Whereas some outside distractions are the result of natural occurrences in life such as the death of a loved one, others result from poor individual decisions such as misdemeanors. In any event, outside distractions can greatly disrupt the continuity of a team by causing team members to focus on external issues unrelated to the team instead of internal goals, such as winning. Whether it's a new romance or a family crisis, outside distractions will inevitably affect all team members at some point in time. High-profile celebrity team members must especially guard against outside distractions due to the magnification of their personal lives in public by media sources. Famous or not, it behooves all team members to make good decisions and understand the impact their actions could have on the rest of the team. Trust me: a team has more than enough potential distractions without additional ones caused by the careless actions of individual team members.

The true test of any team that experiences outside distractions is how well that team handles those distractions as a unit. All teams are affected differently by outside distractions. Some teams pull together and get stronger and even become more efficient in the face of distractions; other teams may become totally distracted, display disunity, exhibit low team morale, or perform poorly. One thing is certain: outside distractions will test the solidarity of even the strongest of teams. That's why communication is key whenever teams are faced with distractions. I'm convinced that if team members know about and understand a particular situation affecting fellow teammates, they will be more willing to rally behind those teammates and show a united front in their efforts to deal with the situation as a team. I know certain issues may be private in nature, but even that can be communicated to the rest of the team. Again, communication is the key!

Ignoring the issues won't make them go away. A team must collectively face its issues and demonstrate a united front in dealing with all outside distractions.

Traditions

The topic of team *traditions* may generate mixed emotions from readers, but it is my belief that traditions can be destructive to teams if they are not properly disseminated within the team concept. Note that not all traditions are necessarily bad. In fact, there are teams that have a winning tradition, which is an absolutely great tradition to have. A tradition of excellence is another great tradition for teams to uphold. However, some other traditions are merely outdated rituals practiced by teams for no apparent reason except to preserve some piece of history. These kinds of traditions can potentially stunt the positive growth of a team over a period of time. Too often traditions become permanent fixtures within teams and their observance is seldom questioned because of their historical relevance. Although they are generally hands-off, I think traditions have to be evaluated case by case to determine whether they are actually helping or hurting the performance progress of a team. Some traditions will have no real effect, good or bad, on a team's performance.

Let's consider the game of football again. Too often I've heard commentators and team members alike refer to their teams as traditional running teams. That's fine, but what happens when you meet an opponent that shuts down your team's running game? Also, what about the team that traditionally plays a one-dimensional quarterback who is either good with his arm or good with his feet but never both? I think some of the best quarterbacks are those who can effectively scramble away from defenders as well as deliver an accurate pass to a receiver. My point is that teams shouldn't allow traditions or traditional practices to solely influence critical decisions that could have huge implications on team success. I understand to a degree that traditions give many team organizations a sense of uniqueness and identity. However, the two fundamental questions teams should ask themselves about traditions are: 1) Which do we value more, our traditions or winning? 2) Do the traditions we faithfully uphold help us or hinder us in our pursuit of becoming a winning team?

To clarify, I'm not talking about traditions such as mascots, team uniforms, game-day rituals, etc. I am referring to traditions of certain practices, procedures, or processes that can adversely affect a team's overall performance. For instance, remember how soldiers fought wars hundreds of years ago by announcing their attacks, standing in a straight line while in plain sight, and letting the enemy take aim to fire shots at them? This traditional style of warfare probably worked great at the time. However, as time progressed, militaries began to realize that winning a battle was best done through the element of surprise. This new paradigm all but eliminated the traditional style of warfare. Similarly, some teams hold on to traditions or traditional practices that worked well in the past but are now ineffective. Teams must always be prepared to make necessary changes for the sake of winning. If traditions can be preserved over time, that's great! However, traditions should never take precedence over winning itself. Again, winning must come first if it's truly the goal of a team. Anything that could potentially hinder a team's chances of winning—including traditions—must be considered for elimination.

Weak Links

You've probably heard before that a team is only as strong as its weakest link. This statement definitely has merit. Weak links do exist among teams, and they come in many forms. They can be people, or they can be procedures or practices carried out by teams. Thus, a weak link is basically anything connected to a team that makes it weak. Competitive teams often look to exploit weak links to aid them in topping their opponents. The good thing about weak links is that they can be addressed. Teams address their weak links in a variety of ways. For instance, some teams try to strengthen or improve their existing weak links through remediation or development, whereas other teams may choose to eliminate their weak links altogether. Each situation is different from team to team.

However, if not addressed, weak links will ultimately weaken the overall performance of a team. People tend to be the most difficult kind of weak link because of our natural resistance to change, even when it's for the best. On several occasions, I've witnessed the power struggle between newly appointed team leaders and old team members who don't want to change their previous mode of operation. They simply like things the way they currently are; they never consider the way things could be. These team members can become weak links because they disrupt team unity and obstruct team progress by not cooperating with the flow of the team. It would be great if team members self-evaluated themselves to see if they were in fact the weak links on the team.

Nevertheless, it behooves all teams to identify and address their weaknesses either through remediation or removal. In either case, teams can't afford to let negative patterns or weaknesses remain intact for long periods of time. Winning teams understand how to quickly resolve their weak-link issues. They essentially fix their weaknesses before they can be detected or exploited by other competitors.

5

The Winning Legacy:
Winning That Keeps On Winning

Winning as a team is truly a great experience, but ask most team members and they'll probably tell you that the next best thing to winning once is winning again and again and again! In short, teams desire long- term winning. However, it doesn't happen instantaneously or overnight. It's a progression for most teams that begins with winning spurts (occasional winning), then goes on to winning streaks (frequent winning), then to winning seasons (sustained winning). And if a team can put together enough winning seasons, it can eventually establish a winning legacy. A winning legacy is long-term winning that's consistently passed down from each generation of teams inside the same team organization. In short, it's inherited winning. This means each newly formed team within a particular organization is expected to uphold that organization's legacy of winning. Needless to say, it takes patience and careful design when building a winning legacy. In this chapter we will explore some important building materials from which winning legacies are created.

Develop a Winning System

Team organizations that establish winning legacies are those that have developed a proven system for winning. A winning system encompasses all the elements and processes that work together efficiently to achieve a team's desired goal of winning. Senior leadership is often tasked with developing a winning system for the entire team organization. Critical decision-making must take place to ensure that all the right elements and processes for winning are put in place. Of course, developing a winning system isn't an exact science. It's more like a work in progress that consists of trial and error. In short, it takes time! Too often, team leaders make the mistake of taking shortcuts when attempting to generate a winning system. For example, some team leaders might observe another team's success and hypothesize that duplicating that team's exact system for winning will automatically translate into success for their teams. This approach almost never works because no two teams are exactly alike, and what works in one team setting may not work in another. That's why winning systems have to be developed, not merely duplicated. Now, don't get me wrong. I'm not saying that teams have to reinvent the wheel in every situation. There are certainly some things that can be duplicated and adapted from one team to another. However, a team must determine which processes are compatible as well as which ones are most feasible to execute.

A winning system must be developed through a series of strategic actions that are carefully planned out and implemented at the most opportune moments. I want to emphasize *most opportune moments* because timing is a crucial component in the development of a winning system. Not all teams have the capacity to implement their strategic-action plans right away. For example, a football team's leadership may decide to implement a new spread-offense as a step toward developing a winning system. However, the successful implementation of this new offense greatly depends on the team's capacity to carry it out. This includes having the right personnel or team members in place to effectively execute the offensive strategy. You see, it doesn't matter how great a system is in theory or design; it can only become a winning system when a team has the capacity to effectively execute it. Nevertheless, once a winning system is developed, winning itself will become self-sustaining, and each new generation of team members will contribute to the continuation of that winning legacy.

Establish a Good Track Record

When building a winning legacy, it's vital for teams to establish a good track record. A team's track record primarily consists of its performance history and perceived reputation as a result thereof. For example, if a team has a history of consistently losing, then its reputation will be perceived as such. It would be hard to recruit quality people to that team because of its reputation of being a losing team. And let's face it, no one really wants to be affiliated with losing. But even a team that has incurred a negative track record has the potential to establish a good one. It may take some time, but it's definitely possible to overcome a negative track record by consistently doing the right things over a period of time. It's also important to note that there can be multiple areas of focus as it relates to establishing a good track record. For instance, a team may have a good track record in performance, but a poor track record in ethics. Too often we see a team's winning track record overshadowed by ethics violations or scandals. Any time a team is accused of misconduct, cheating, or having an unfair advantage in order to win, the reputation of the team's program is diminished. Whether it's in the area of recruiting, marketing, performance, ethics, or public relations, winning teams understand the importance of establishing a good track record in *all* areas and the significance it plays in attracting quality people to their teams. Teams that establish good track records seem to have a continual supply of quality recruits year after year. On the other hand, it's hard to recruit quality team members to a team with a poor track record, especially in winning.

Now that we understand the need for establishing a good track record, let's briefly consider how it's done. There is a term that should be the foundation for all teams desiring to establish a good track record and ultimately a winning legacy: best practices. The phrase itself may seem self-explanatory, but it means different things for different teams. I would describe best practices as proven and effective ways of carrying out specific tasks, assignments, functions, and processes within a team organization. Best practices are standards that all teams should strive toward in every facet of their operations. It's also important to note that best practices are either acquired or adapted by teams. For example, some teams *acquire* best practices through trial and error. They simply learn the right way to execute tasks based on multiple attempts that have failed to produce the desired results in a particular area. Other teams simply *adapt* the best practices of other teams or notable sources that have already acquired certain best practices over time. Whether acquired or adapted, best practices help teams establish impeccable track records and reinforce a standard of excellence that entices people to be a part of their organizations.

In addition to best practices, teams should always recruit individual team members who have good track records themselves. Why hire a coach with a losing track record? Why hire a teacher who gets fired from a different school every year? Why recruit a player with a history of negative behavior? I pose these questions because individual track records do matter in the overall scheme of establishing a good team track record. In any case, once teams are committed to establishing a good track record through best practices and a standard of excellence, then the win potential for those teams will dramatically increase.

Implement the 3 Rs of Winning

The success of any team organization in establishing a winning legacy is largely due to its ability to recruit, rehab, and release team members on a *continual basis*. It's a cycle that I'd like to call the 3 Rs of winning.

Let's begin with the first R, recruiting. The recruiting process of a team is much like the restocking process of a store. Stores have to periodically restock their shelves with items to prevent a supply shortage. Likewise, teams have to periodically restock themselves with quality team members to prevent a shortage in winning. This analogy demonstrates the importance of timing as it relates to the recruiting process. Recruiting should never begin after all or most of the quality team members have departed the team. No, recruiting should be an ongoing process based on future projections of a team's needs prior to them arising. In the business world, companies strive to have no break in services. Similarly, teams should strive to have no break in winning.

Teams that establish winning legacies understand that the purpose of recruiting is to ensure success in winning for consecutive years – not just the here and now. When there's a break in winning, it's usually because teams are inconsistent in recruiting quality individuals or perhaps late in developing new recruits to replace outgoing team members. When teams experience a losing season immediately after a winning season, many explain the phenomenon as being the team's "growth season." However, if recruiting is done properly, there should be new recruits always growing, developing, and getting hands-on experience prior to occupying prominent positions of outgoing team members. As a result, new recruits will be better equipped to step right into those positions and do what's required to maintain the team's winning legacy.

The second R of winning is rehabbing. After being on a team for some time, a recruited team member can eventually lose some of the performance attributes that once made him or her invaluable to the team. If and when this happens, teams usually make an attempt to rehabilitate the team member in question. Rehabbing encompasses a team's effort to restore a team member's proper functioning in a specified role or position. In other words, if a team member's performance is not up to par, then the team as a unit will work with that member to get him or her back on track. Sometimes rehabbing involves peer-to-peer mentoring; sometimes special training in a particular area is needed. Whatever the method may be, it is crucial for the team members in question to enter the rehab process with openness, honesty, and willingness to work on their areas of weakness that have been identified. Needless to say, patience and support is needed from everyone on the team during this process. Finally, a team's leadership must evaluate the rehabilitation process to see if team members are truly making progress.

Ultimately, low-performing team members must not be allowed to compromise the overall performance of a team. If it is determined that a team member can't perform at a desired level after having spent an appropriate length of time in rehab, then the team's leadership will likely have to explore the option of releasing that member from the team.

In fact, the last R needed to ensure a team's winning legacy is called releasing. It will always be necessary to release team members from teams for various reasons. Most often, team members must be released due to performance-related issues. Although talent and ability can indeed diminish with age, the physical condition of an individual isn't the only reason for unsatisfactory performance. Sometimes internal team conflicts, outside distractions, and a host of other issues affect the performance of team members. Most teams will allow their members a grace period to make improvements before considering their release. Rehabbing usually takes place during this grace period. However, if there is no significant improvement in performance over this period of time, then leadership must decide whether to continue with rehab efforts or to simply release the team member for the greater good. Teams must exercise balance when releasing team members. Releasing too many team members in a short period of time (a high turnover rate) can communicate trouble to onlookers.

In some cases, team members have to be released for issues unrelated to performance. For instance, a team member may join another team to gain a better opportunity or a promotion. Team members are also traded and recruited by other teams at will. Therefore, teams should be prepared for the release of current team members by constantly recruiting and developing new members. Ultimately, winning teams know how and when to release team members in order to maintain their winning legacies.

Change with Game Changers

In time, all team organizations will eventually be confronted with the element of change. For some teams, change is easy, yet for others change is difficult. For winning teams, change is a necessity and has little to do with the comfort level of the change itself. In the world of winning there will always be game changers that prompt teams to respond with changes of their own to sustain long-term winning. I remember, for example, when hamburger restaurants served nothing but hamburgers. Today, some of those same restaurants offer chicken, salad, dessert, breakfast, and toys. This is due to certain game changers which, over time, caused businesses in the food industry to change their approach to winning sales over the competition. With the rise of the one-stop shop paradigm, many businesses began to offer a wide range of products under one roof to prevent their customers from spending money at other more specialized stores. Another example of a game changer is the emergence of technology. The Internet alone has changed the game for many team-based companies and organizations that participate in e-commerce. The potential to reach clientele all over the world is fascinating and mind-boggling, yet many organizations are still content to do business as usual without participating in modern technology. My point is that teams must be versatile enough to change with game changers as they occur over time. Remember, it's not a matter of *"if"* game changers will occur, but it's a matter of *"when"*. Winning teams that establish winning legacies demonstrate the ability to successfully change with game changers as they occur. The evolutionary concept of survival of the fittest suggests that the most fit species are the ones that survive environmental changes over time by successfully adapting to them. I believe this analogy captures the essence of winning teams that sustain winning by adapting to game changers that occur over time.

Additionally, teams can introduce game changers of their own by being innovative and creative. It's imperative that teams never become stagnated in their current success. A common temptation for teams is to keep doing the same things that helped them initially become successful. That's perfectly understandable, and to a degree, a good philosophy. However, if a team doesn't meet game changers with corresponding changes, the team jeopardizes its chances to sustain the kind of long-term winning that produces winning legacies. Teams that understand the need to win also understand the need to change. Finally, winning teams never see change as a hindrance to progress, but rather, as a necessary tool in the construction of a winning legacy.

Stay Innovative and Creative

The greatest challenge for many winning teams that make it to the top is figuring out how to stay there! Most teams that establish winning legacies do so by staying on the cutting edge of progress and performance. Since winning with longevity is the basis for establishing a winning legacy, teams must constantly employ strategies that will keep them winning in their particular arenas. One of the ways that teams can sustain long-term winning is by staying innovative and creative. Through innovation and creativity, winning teams are able to cultivate new, effective, and relevant ways of winning. Innovative and creative teams are like rivers, always advancing and moving forward. In contrast, teams that get too lackadaisical and stagnant are like pond water. Instead of moving forward in innovation and creativity, these teams simply stand still and become stuck in a cycle of outdated routines. Teams that are innovative and creative definitely know how to operate outside of the box.

I believe all teams need some type of X factor that sets them apart from the rest of the competition. For instance, as a hotelier, what amenities can you offer your guests that will give you the edge over the competition? Is it state-of-the-art facilities, full breakfast, or a spa? Whatever it is, it should cause your organization to stand out from the rest of the hotel competition. On the side of innovation, teams should look to pioneer new or groundbreaking ideas to stay on top of their competition. Also, teams shouldn't underestimate the power of creativity. Creativity is a powerful tool that allows many teams to recycle their current resources and stay ahead of the competition. When teams are outmatched financially by their competition, creativity can be a cost-effective way to produce competitive results. Whereas a team's budget may be limited, there's no limitation on creativity. Additionally, teams don't always have to create their own tools for success. In a world of emerging technologies and social media, organizations can and should take advantage of the innovation and creativity of others. Some teams are only one blog, one video, one website, or perhaps one e-newsletter away from surpassing their competition. That's why it's important for teams who aspire to win to stay current, relevant, and on the cutting edge of progress by being innovative and creative.

Keep a Team-Over-Talent Philosophy

One essential for winning teams establishing winning legacies is the ability to keep a team-over-talent philosophy year after year. The talent pool represented by individuals on a team is certainly important in the general scheme of winning, so it's not uncommon to emphasize talent or highlight talented individuals on a team. However, I think trouble comes when too much emphasis is placed on talent. A team should place its emphasis or primary focus on the overall well-being of the team. Talent is only one aspect of a team and doesn't account for the totality of an exceptional team performance. In short, talent can only take a team so far. I believe a winning team is the ultimate result of total team success and not just individual talent. If talent alone was responsible for winning results, then there would be no need for leadership, systems, game plans, practices, accountability, etc. That's why it's critical to guard the team concept and prevent talent or talented individuals from taking preeminence over the team. When recruiting talented individuals for a team, recruiters should be just as interested in a prospect's character and ability to work well with others. Remember, the best fit for a team is an individual who fits best inside the team concept. If a team member is talented yet disruptive to the team concept, then he or she is a liability.

That's why I have the utmost respect for team leaders who uphold a team-over-talent philosophy. These are the types of leaders who will sideline a star team member just to send a clear message to the rest of the team. That message, of course, is that there is nothing more important than preserving the unity, integrity, and chemistry of the team. I think team leaders take a huge gamble when they exalt talent above the team. Team-over-talent is about having a standard that doesn't conveniently change to appease select individuals. In a team-over-talent economy, no one is given a free pass; all team members must follow the same guidelines. No partiality or favoritism is shown. Teams that establish winning legacies do so by preserving a strong team concept year after year. This includes getting buy-in from each team member and solidifying an overwhelming commitment to the idea of team.

6

The Winning Outcome:
Evidence of Victory through Planning,
Preparing, and Performing

Purpose in Planning

Any team organization that charts its success based on winning will never be content with losing. The whole idea is to
win—yet winning isn't the result of some whimsical, magical
intervention. No, winning is the result of a well-designed
plan that is purposeful and intentional with ramifications for
being well executed. Some teams omit the planning process
altogether; consequently, losses will occur. Take the airline
industry, for example. A great deal of planning takes place
on several different levels to ensure safe flying to various
destinations. Suppose a pilot decides to just take off in an

airplane full of people with no planned route or destination. This ill-advised journey would likely be chaotic, resulting in lost time, energy, resources, and potentially, lives, all due to failure in planning. Although this scenario is unlikely, there are certainly teams that theoretically take the same approach to winning. They simply take off on a journey to win with no real plan. During the journey, these teams waste valuable time and resources by circling the runway of their success; they simply don't know how or where to land into it.

In the middle of performing is not the time to consider planning. Planning should always precede performance. One cliché states that poor planning produces poor performances. I certainly agree. There is a definite link between good planning and good performance. Teams that employ good planning better position themselves for favorable outcomes. That's not to say that there won't be unexpected occurrences, but having a good plan in place increases the chances of things going right during a performance.

Good planning is also strategic planning. Strategic planning is planning with purpose. Once the ultimate goal of winning is established, strategic planning assists teams in identifying ideas, strategies, steps, objectives, and timelines to accomplish that goal. Let's suppose a team was in a strategic planning session with a professional consultant. The session would probably involve brainstorming to generate ideas about the ultimate goal of winning. Since winning means different things to different teams, the term "winning" would have to be specified for that particular team. The team's leadership might also be required to formulate a vision statement and/or a mission statement prior to or during the session to connect purpose to the overall goal. Additionally, the consultant would likely ask team members to identify areas of focus that need improvement, enhancement, or expansion. Time would also have to be taken into consideration. As the saying goes, Rome wasn't built in a day. Therefore, many strategic plans can have a three- to five- year projection. In any case, the whole objective of the strategic planning session is to develop a concrete plan for reaching the desired goal. Teams with vague ideas or no real plan of to how to reach their desired goals will have difficulty in obtaining them.

During the planning phase, teams should definitely do their homework! In other words, teams should research various aspects of a plan prior to implementing them. A plan may look good on paper, but it also has to be feasible for a particular team to execute. What good is it to make a plan that the team can't collectively execute? The purpose of planning is to ensure that teams operate with the efficiency needed to win. Think of it this way: planning affects execution, and execution affects performance, and performance affects a team's winning outcome. All teams must develop a concrete plan for their success, whether they do it in-house or through an outside professional. It may not be the most exciting aspect of developing a winning team, but planning is certainly one of the most important ones.

Preparing to Perform

After a team organization has completed planning toward a winning outcome, the next phase is to preparing to perform. Preparing for a performance can involve a number of extensive details. These details represent countless variations and combinations of things that teams must do to prepare themselves for a performance situation. No two teams are exactly alike; there will be distinguishing factors that determine how particular teams prepare for their performances. Those factors could be influenced by leadership styles, current resources, and other team dynamics. The goal of a team's preparation time is to produce the best performance outcome possible. Instead of trying to list every minute detail of preparation, I thought it would be more beneficial to discuss three important areas of preparation that teams need to address in order to perform with efficiency and excellence.

I. Preparation through Capacity Building

Sometimes the plans of a team can be realistic and doable just not realistic to do right now! This is because there are times when teams aren't readily equipped, have the capacity, to perform at certain levels. Think of it this way: an eight-ounce glass can't contain two gallons of water. The volume of the glass doesn't have the capacity to contain more than eight ounces of water. Therefore, the capacity of the glass must be increased to perform the job of containing two gallons of water. Similarly, teams can only perform at levels for which they have the capacity. They must strategically enlarge their capacities to perform at higher levels of competitiveness. For example, if a print shop can only print a small volume due to limited team members and equipment, then that particular shop may also be limited in the level at which it can compete for clientele. The particular shop would have to acquire additional people and equipment to build its capacity in order to perform larger print jobs. Preparation through capacity building has to do with teams acquiring what they need to get a performance job done. It's important to note that teams can build capacity either internally or externally. For instance, a team can build its capacity by acquiring needed resources that exist outside of what it currently has (external), or it can build its capacity from within by cultivating resources it already has (internal). In either case, the main objective of capacity building is to increase team efficiency for a better overall performance.

2. Preparation through Development

Let's assume each member of a team is fully functional and free of any impairment. Each one would be expected to effectively carry out his or her assigned tasks. Although this is a reasonable expectation, there are times when team members need additional development to effectively carry out their assigned tasks. This development generally takes place through training sessions, workshops, practice, and courses. The objective of development is to maximize the ability of each team member to perform at his or her highest degree of effectiveness. It's futile to expect an exceptional performance from underdeveloped team members. That's why many organizations provide ongoing development for their team members. For example, if a school system wants to implement the newest classroom technology, then the system will provide professional development training to ensure all its team members are ready to perform effectively with the new technology. It's only fair to equip team members for the jobs they are expected to do.

A big misconception about development is that something is wrong with the individuals who need it. In fact, if a team member can be developed it means he or she is still valuable and capable of performing tasks on behalf of the team. On the other hand, if a team member can't be developed, then he or she probably won't be on the team much longer. Constant changes that affect team systems over time will always demand the development of team members. Development should be viewed as a vehicle for growth towards achieving maximum productivity in every performance situation.

3. Preparation through Internal Controls and Accountability

Winning teams, like good computers, have good operating systems. This means that winning teams have efficient, systematic ways of carrying out various team procedures, tasks, and responsibilities. A good operating system doesn't work just because a team wants it to. Certain mechanisms must be put in place to ensure that teams and their members operate with the consistency, efficiency, and effectiveness required for victory. One such mechanism is internal controls. Internal controls usually refer to financial accountability practices within businesses. The term can also be applied within the context of a team. Thus, internal controls provide teams with guidelines, standards, and accountability for how various tasks and procedures are. Moreover, they represent specific practices put in place to ensure there are checks and balances within a particular organization. Essentially, internal controls help prevent the abuse of power or position by defining who does what, when, and how.

When preparing for a performance it's important for all team members to know their individual roles and responsibilities. It's also important that team members be held accountable for carrying out those roles and responsibilities efficiently. In short, everyone must know their lanes and stay inside them. In the absence of internal controls and accountability, any lane can be crossed, resulting in team members colliding with each other-wrecking the team. That's why accountability in the form of adequate, impartial supervision is needed on all levels of a team organization. This will ensure that team members maximize their productivity in preparation for an exceptional team performance.

Performing for Victory

The driving force behind any team victory is the relentless desire to win. This relentless desire causes teams to take all necessary paths to generate a winning performance. This includes making tough but important decisions in the best interests of the team. It also means that teams are willing to make necessary adjustments during a performance situation to increase their chances of winning. This is important because things don't always go as planned, especially in live performance situations. At times even go-to team members can be off or less productive when performing. Because there are no guarantees in a performance situation, making necessary adjustments is critical to a team's success. However, making these adjustments can only be effective when team members embrace flexibility. For instance, a superstar team member may have to sacrifice his or her own opportunity to shine for a fellow teammate to emerge as a key contributor to the team's victory. Again, the key word is *adjustment*. It frightens me when team members are so rigid in their roles that they can't be flexible enough to function in other capacities when their teams need them to.

Team members who are dedicated to winning will sacrifice their own comfort for victory. Sometimes, this means participating in value shifts that can occur within teams. A value shift has to do with reassigning the value of team members by making changes to their statuses, functions, or positions in order to leverage team strengths in other areas. Let's say a team member flourishes in a particular role on a team for a season. When that season is over, the team may opt to shift that team member to another capacity in order to preserve the value or valuable contributions of that team member. These types of adjustments may be needed to positively impact a team's overall performance. That's what performing for victory is all about. Teams have to be willing to do what it takes (legally and ethically) to win, which means producing an exceptional performance through a win-driven approach to every performance situation.

Performance Measures

Performance measures aid teams in pursuing the ultimate goal of winning. Performance measures are ways to measure a team's performance across various areas. Since winning is largely predicated upon giving an exceptional performance, it's important for teams to evaluate their performances. The old cliché, "What doesn't get measured, doesn't get done," is the premise for establishing performance measures. If teams don't measure or evaluate their own performances, it will be difficult for them to know whether they are progressing toward victory. It will also be difficult to pinpoint problem areas and improve them. Basically, performance measures help teams identify what they should be doing in order to win.

It's important to note that performance measures are usually determined by a team's performance results. When those results are properly evaluated, teams are able to identify focus areas for improvement as well as to solidify performance objectives. Additionally, performance measures can be both *quantitative* and *qualitative* in nature. Quantitative performance measures are based upon numbers, figures, or percentages, whereas qualitative performance measures are based upon observations and descriptions. For example, a quantitative performance measure could track the number of sales in a quarter. A qualitative performance measure could observe how well team members interact with each other as they complete certain tasks. Both quantitative and qualitative performance measures are valid tools that can be used to help teams effectively evaluate their performances.

When performance measures are determined, there must be accountability to ensure team members are progressing toward their expected performance levels. This accountability often comes in the form of *progress monitoring*. Progress monitoring is a systematic evaluation process that involves collecting performance information through checkups, observations, reports, and evaluations. The information gathered through progress monitoring provides accountability as well as incentive for team members to effectively execute their assigned tasks. It also provides feedback to team leaders on their team's progress in various performance areas.

Additionally, progress monitoring helps teams remain aligned with their performance objectives. Whenever performance objectives need to be reached on a certain timeline, *benchmarks* are often used as sub-goals to track the rate of progress toward the ultimate goal. Benchmarks are like mile-markers on the journey to exceptional team performance. They are important to performance measurement because if a team lags behind in making timely progress in a particular performance area, then some type of intervention must be introduced to get the team on track with its performance objectives.

All of these components of performance measures work together to give teams a good picture of their current performance status. Lastly, it's important for teams to eliminate abstract theories for success and focus concretely on what will lead them to an exceptional performance and ultimately success in winning.

7

The Challenge

Congratulations! Now that you've successfully navigated the concepts of this victory guide, I want to encourage you to continue your pursuit of winning. I trust that this book will become one of many tools you use to propel you and your team to a greater level of success in winning. Before I conclude, I want to leave you with a few challenges to cement your successful completion of this book.

Challenge #1: Do a self-evaluation.

Go back through the book and highlight any specifics that apply directly to you or your team. Take note of those areas, especially the unhealthy ones, and strategically address them. Remember: it's hard to treat something that hasn't been diagnosed!

Challenge #2: Act now.

If you have a deep conviction that your team can, should, and will become a better team—a winning team—then don't wait for some magical event to transform your team. No, take the destiny of your team into your own hands and do all you can to help improve your team day by day.

Challenge #3: Do your homework.

Some research is required on your team's journey to success in winning. Whether it's learning the practices of other successful organizations or acquiring team-centered literature, you must be willing to research and tap into other available resources and venues to help your team win.

Challenge #4: Don't focus on the past.

I challenge you to look ahead with a fearless ambition to succeed. Don't focus on past failures or even past successes. I want you to look ahead to greater heights and achievements, both for you and your team!

Challenge #5: Stay positive and optimistic.

No matter where your team may find itself on the winning spectrum, it's important to always stay positive and optimistic about the opportunity to become better. Things might seem to get worse before they get better. However, keeping a positive and optimistic attitude will ensure the possibility of an eventual turnaround for your team. It's easy to be down and negative if winning has evaded your team for some time now. I challenge you to take the high road and stay positive and optimistic. Now, although you haven't found the path to winning yet, you have definitely found the path to losing! Therefore, utilize the knowledge of what hasn't worked for your team in order to propel you in the direction of what will work. Again, the key is to stay positive and optimistic!

Conclusion

As you and your team continue to embark upon the journey of success in winning, always believe in your collective abilities to capture success and become extraordinary in this season. I believe this victory guide will be a great asset in helping to propel your team beyond the gravitational pull of mediocrity. As you continue to ingest the principles of this book, I hope this reading experience proves to be a moment of demarcation in your team organization. Finally, it is my hope that this victory guide will serve as a continuous resource for positive growth in overall team performance and as a catalyst for average teams to ultimately become winning teams!

About the Author

Sederick Fluker is a prolific writer, teacher, and success coach. He is an Alabama native whose passion is to help others reach their full potential. Sederick's life has been a legacy of leadership and community service. His service-oriented projects have earned him numerous honors and awards such as Community Leader of the Year, and he was inducted into the prestigious organization Leadership Montgomery. Sederick holds a bachelor's degree in Education, a master's degree in Counseling, and a Family Development Credential (FDC) for his work empowering families in need. He has been an educator in a public school, a counselor and mentor to at-risk youth, and the executive director of a nonprofit organization.

www.ingramcontent.com/pod-product-compliance
Lightning Source LLC
Chambersburg PA
CBHW022102170526
45157CB00004B/1446